IF THEY WANT TO…
THEY GONE TO

THE POWER TO CHOOSE

By
Shavon A. Hampton

Novahs Publishing

NOVAHS PUBLISHING

Published by Novahs Publishing LLC.

Scriptures used are from King James Version (KJV)

Large Print Edition Copyright 2016

by Christian Art Publishing.

DEDICATION

—◆—

To my younger self. I would not know what
I know now, nor would I be where I am today
if it had not been for your resilience. Just so
you know, you were always enough. You were
fearfully and wonderfully made!
Just wait and see!

To the readers for beginning this journey
with me. Let's make magic!

TABLE OF CONTENTS

————◆————

FOREWARD

This author has always been the child with great potential. As I have watched her from a bud, she has opened and bloomed from her trials and tribulations to the voice you will hear as she bravely opens her heart to every reader. This book is not for the weak of heart, but it's a must-read for all those who are seeking a place to spread out their secrets and embrace the process of healing. If you are caught

> *This book is not for the weak of heart, but it's a must-read for all those who are seeking a place to spread out their secrets and embrace the process of healing.*

in the snares of broken promises and have developed scars gathered during the search for your "Happily Ever After," this book is for you. If you have been left wounded by the wayside but are still mustering up the strength to expose the secrets hidden deep within, this book is for you. As you open your heart, allow yourself to receive the revelation by which transformation will come. Remember, it's a process. I am so proud of her as a woman as she embarks on this new adventure with

> *As you open your heart, allow yourself to receive the revelation by which transformation will come.*

courage and fortitude. She steps into another level of discovering her powers within. She is the youngest of my three daughters, although we share a dual role. I will always be her mother, but she is also my friend, as I am hers. I cherish the relationship that we have developed as she matures and soars.

Rev. Gwendolyn Hampton

INTRODUCTION

*"Whoso findeth a wife findeth a good thing,
and obtaineth favour of the LORD."*

~ PROVERBS 18:22

This book is for people at a crossroad in their lives, whether male or female, young or seasoned. The fact is that adversities will definitely come in life. The true test is in how you handle that storm. Will you fold in the face of the storm, or will you withstand the winds? Even when it hurts. And guess what? Life doesn't stop just because the storm is in town. So how do you manage both—

> *The true test is in how you handle that storm. Will you fold in the face of the storm, or will you withstand the winds?*

life and the storm? Better yet, how do you handle life after the storm? Just like with a death, you have to grieve while maintaining daily tasks. Not only that but you also have to put the pieces back together again in the aftermath. It is an uphill journey to healing after adversities are thrown in your path. Whether they be little pebbles or big boulders, they are all a nuisance. My hope is for readers not just to read this book but also to experience this book. I hope that each and every word creates a different experience for each and every reader. My vision is to give you the feeling of an intimate

> *With each new stage comes a different perspective*

conversation with your best friend. Don't be afraid to talk back to me and to jot down responses and notes on the pages! Read this book as many times as you deem necessary! I think this message may be helpful in different stages of your ever-evolving journey. With each new stage comes a different perspective. Let's begin this journey together!

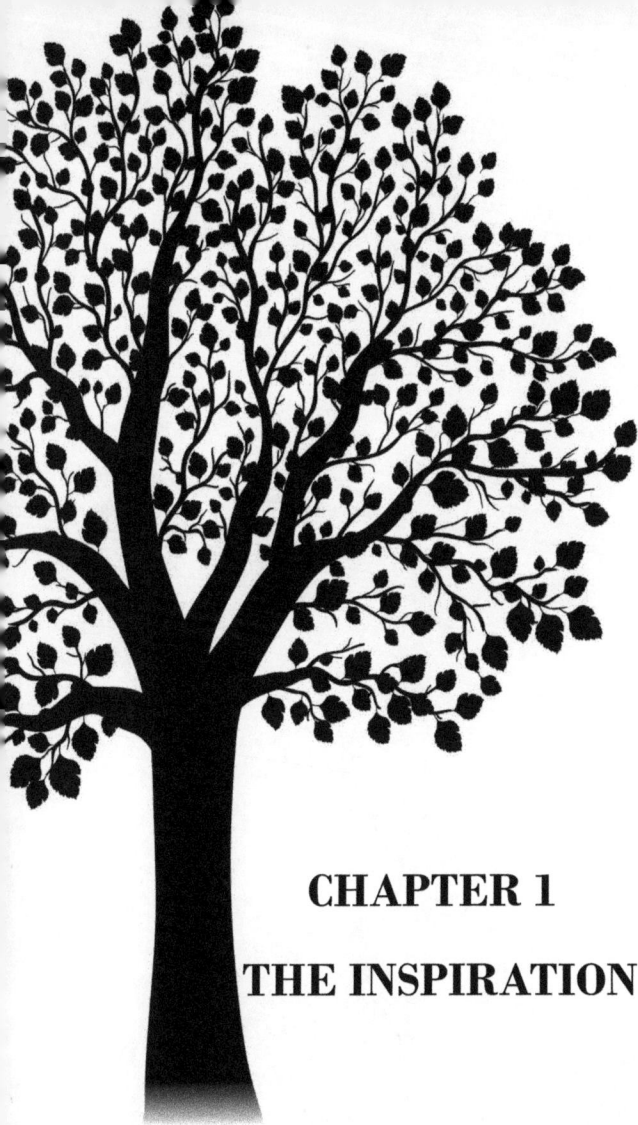

CHAPTER 1

THE INSPIRATION

"And we know that all things work together for good to them that love God, to them who are the called according to His purpose."

~ Romans 8:28

The inspiration for this book originally came from a casual conversation with a group of friends about men cheating. **"If they want to… they gone to"** was my stance on that topic. My position was that there is nothing a woman can do to stop a man from cheating if that's what he really wants to do. Cooking three full-course meals a day, keeping your body tight, being a lady in the streets and a you-know-what in the sheets will not stop him. At that time, I had recently gotten out of a 15-year adulterous marriage. Most people thought that we had it made. For a young black couple to last 15 years during this day and time, they

> *My position was that there is nothing a woman can do to stop a man from cheating if that's what he really wants to do.*

were thought to be out of the danger zone of getting a divorce. No matter what was going on behind closed doors. No matter if the couple was actually happy. No matter if the husband beat his wife. No matter if the couple slept in separate bedrooms and were merely cohabiting. If their mail was delivered to the same address and

> *No matter what was going on behind closed doors. No matter if the couple was actually happy.*

they shared the same last name for that length of time, it was viewed as winning the gold medal in the Olympics of relationships.

In the beginning, I thought I had it all. I knew he wasn't a model citizen, but I felt that he was a good provider. We were homeowners at a young age, we had decent cars, took decent trips, had good kids, etc. So we lived a good and decent life as average adults—or so I thought. Sooo...most adults dealt with adultery at some point of their marriage. What I was going through was nothing out of the norm...right?

Well, to my surprise, I began to feel ashamed when I spoke aloud what I had been through, what I had dealt with. As the old saying goes, "If it don't sound right when you say

What I was going through was nothing out of the norm...right?

it out loud, then it prob'ly ain't right."

I guess, looking at it with a different set of eyes, I realized how disrespectful and degrading being married to a serial cheater actually was. It's something that you never forget. As a matter of fact, you are always trying to overcome the residue of the damage that was caused by this behavior. It's a form of violation. You may have been too naïve to fight against it at that time, but when you realize that you were in fact violated, you deal with that pain all over again—now in a different way, because you have a name for it.

At that time my thought process was, "If he's going to cheat, he better respect me enough to not let me find out." You see, I believed that 9.5 times out of 10, a man was going to cheat. Growing up as a teenager, that was what I knew to be true of men. On the radio they sang about it. In the movies they portrayed it. Music videos reenacted scenarios of a

> *I was blind to the fact that cheating itself is disrespectful!*

man trying to juggle two women at a time and ultimately getting caught. My own beloved dad had done it.

So there was nothing around me saying anything different, other than **men will be unfaithful**; but if they love you, they will respect you and always come home and provide a good life for you. I was blind to the fact that cheating itself is disrespectful! That entire frame of thinking deserves a completely separate book.

If we are really being honest—I know I can be honest with you—I accepted the behavior at that time for a lot of different reasons that we will uncover later in this book. I felt like that was what I deserved. Crazy, huh? I may not have

> *No matter how good of a thing nor how bad of a thing, ultimately, if you want to…you gone to!*

said it. I may not have even known it, but the feeling was there, somewhere deep in my soul. So deep, that it went unrecognized for decades.

After this initial conversation, I realized that the "if they want to…they gone to" concept covers basically any and all areas of life. That's something to think about! If you think about it realistically, what will you do that you have absolutely no desire to do? Nothing! On the flip side of the coin, if you really want to do a thing, there is nothing that will stop you. No matter how good of a thing nor how bad of a thing, ultimately, **if *you* want to…you gone to!** Let's chat about it.

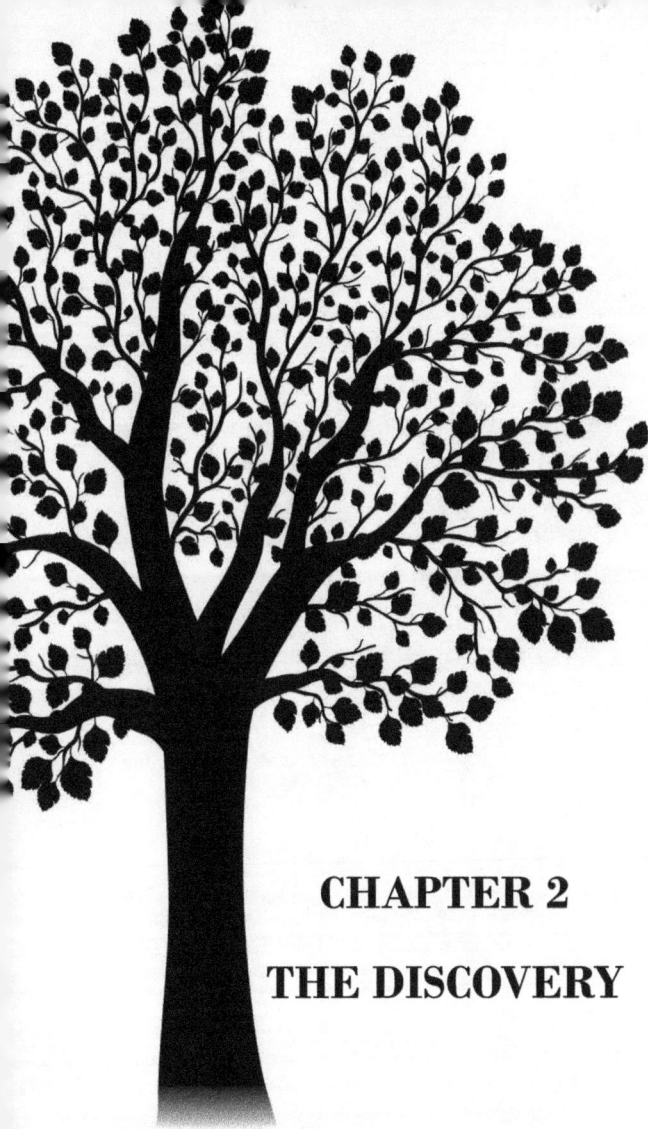

CHAPTER 2

THE DISCOVERY

*"And He said unto them, he that hath ears
to hear, let him hear."*

~ MARK 4:9

As children, many of us were told by someone at some point in our lives, "You can do whatever that you put in your mind to do." Usually you would hear this in a graduation message in some shape or form, whether it's a kindergarten graduation or a college graduation. That is the ultimate motivation for a new grad to realize their full potential and to give them

> *"You can do whatever that you put in your mind to do."*

the boost needed after their long journey as they move forward in their life into the next stage of their education or as a new professional.

Motivational phrases are used in all types of media. They are used in movies, such as in *The Help*: "You is smart, you is kind, and you is

23

important." It's a form of affirmation to motivate and encourage. They are used by songwriters in their songs, such as DJ Khaled: "You smart, you real smart." There are pages on Pinterest dedicated to motivational quotes and phrases. The intention is to instill confidence where there may be a lack thereof.

The word "motivate," according to my personal assistant Google, means to "provide (someone) with a motive for doing something." Sometimes we need a reminder that we are capable of what may seem like the impossible. That's when motivation of some sort can

> *The intention is to instill confidence where there may be a lack thereof.*

swoop in and save the day. It can make us feel like Superman or Wonder Woman. The right motivation at the right time can shift your entire mood, which, in turn, will change your action, which can then change your day, which will then put you on track to a life change.

Well, this quote is one that I like to call a **reality quote**. It sums up the majority of all of the best of the best motivational quotes. Think about it: what is the underlying message? You can do anything that in your heart of hearts you really desire to do—in other words, that **if you want to...you gone to!**

Your brain will literally not allow you to do something if you have categorized it as something that you do not want to do. When you try to complete the task, your brain will fight against your body, or other thoughts will come to mind that will

> *Your brain will literally not allow you to do something if you have categorized it as something that you do not want to do.*

take precedence over that task. For example, if you sign up with a new personal trainer (which is good, right?) in hopes that spending the money will serve as your motivation, but you tell yourself en route (this is where you go wrong) to your very first session, "He ain't gonna have me doing this or that"—that is sending your brain the message that those particular things are the enemy. So when you are asked to do the very thing that you had just told yourself on the ride over that you were not going to do (because you will probably be asked to do that exact thing), your brain will sense the panic and go into

> *Now you are hyper-ventilating, vomiting, and sweating like you are in Death Valley, California, in mid-July.*

combat mode. Now you are hyper-ventilating, vomiting, and sweating like you are in Death Valley, California, in mid-July. Now when you think of the gym, you have this negative connotation in mind. Actually what happened was that you focused so much on why you should not work out—although you purposely paid your good hard-earned money with the hopes of psyching yourself into enjoying what you have deemed unenjoyable—and this negative focus manifested right before your eyes.

This is a powerful revelation, right?! Think about that for a second! You told yourself what you were not going to do, almost as a dare. *Am I strong enough to stick to my own word?* That little thought can sneak

> *You told yourself what you were not going to do, almost as a dare.*

in, in the midst of the conversation that you held with yourself in the car, playing like elevator music in the background, almost unknowingly. It was so vague that you quickly forgot the thought.

What else can the mind conjure up? What will it store in its back storeroom that we have forgotten was placed there? What have you told yourself, or maybe even just thought to yourself but did not share with anyone? Maybe it was something told to you by someone whose opinion you held as valuable? What did you do with that thought? Where did you place it? Is it in that dusty back storeroom, placed in the corner in a box that sits on top of a much larger box? That storeroom can be thought of as the subconscious mind, the part of the mind that stores our thoughts and unknowingly controls our actions. The subconscious mind is what is ultimately the driving force behind the idea that "if they want to...they gone to."

As previously mentioned, this reality quote can be used in a positive or a negative light. Some negative ways include:

1. If someone desires to be dishonest, no matter how much they know that they should not...they will.

> *If someone desires to be dishonest, no matter how much they know that they should not...they will.*

2. If someone wants to sleep in, no matter what type of deadlines they may have...they will.

3. If someone chooses to commit adultery, no matter how much of a good family they have...they will.

4. If someone commits to following Satan, no matter how much of God's Word they may know...they will.

5. If someone elects to adopt a hateful spirit, no matter how kind others are to them...they will.

If you notice, the words that proceed "someone" in the above list are descriptions of some form of choice. "Want," "desire," "choose,"

> *"Want," "desire," "choose," "commit," and "elect" are all words that require the will to do, to carry it out.*

"commit," and "elect" are all words that require the will to do, to carry it out. "Will" by definition is "a strong desire or determination to do something," according to *The Merriam-Webster Dictionary*. Merriam-Webster's definition of "determination" is "a quality that makes you continue trying to do or achieve something that is difficult; the act of officially deciding something."

I would like to pause on that word "determination" for a moment. That is such a powerful word. With determination, you can move a mountain! With determination, a 5-foot, 100-pound woman would fight off a baby bear to save her child. With determination, an abused mother would have the courage to leave her abuser. With determination, that high school dropout can obtain a GED. With

> *With determination, a dying father will fight off death long enough to see his long-lost child make it to his side.*

determination, a dying father will fight off death long enough to see his long-lost child make it to his side. Determination will allow you to finally follow your dreams and do what you have been too afraid to do.

At some point, we may choose to adopt fear and lose our determination. What would it take for you to achieve your wildest dream? That dream that you feel could **only** be a dream. That dream that is so big that you can't even think of the first step that will lead you in the right direction. Maybe you dream of having your artwork on display at the Louvre, the largest museum in the world, located in Paris, France. That's a huge dream with many steps to accom-

> *That dream that is so big that you can't even think of the first step that will lead you in the right direction*

plish the end goal. **It only takes action to get started!** The sheer determination **to make the first step toward the first step**. You may say that it's easier said than done, which is true. But at some point the choice will be made either to follow the road of your determination or to follow the road of your fear. **If you want to…you gone to!**

Back to the word "will." Remember, by definition it means "a strong desire or determination
to do something." So "will" and "determination"
go hand-in-hand. The will is the feeling or desire you have that
makes you act. The
act is your determi-
nation. Your will
can work in positive ways as well as negative,
much like determination. Some positive exam-
ples of a strong will include:

> *The will is the feeling or desire you have that makes you act.*

1. If someone desires to be honest, no matter
how easy it would be to lie...they will.

2. If someone wants to awaken before the
chickens, no matter how much they want to
sleep in...they will.

3. If someone chooses to stay faithful
to their family, no matter how they are
tempted...they will.

4. If someone elects to adopt kindness, no matter how rude others are to them…they will.

This raises a question: Who are you at your core? What is in your heart? As the Bible says in Luke 6:45, "For it is out of the abundance

> *This raises a question: Who are you at your core? What is in your heart?*

of the heart that the mouth speaks." Your words become your actions, and that is what people will remember most about you. Again I ask, **who are you at your core? What is in your heart?** Your will causes you to become determined enough to do a thing.

Let's further examine an example—both the negative side of the coin and the positive side of the coin.

1. Negative Perspective: If someone desires to be dishonest—say a close friend lies and asks you to vouch for them and you agree—that means that you are co-signing their lie and thus you are also lying. It may be easy because you don't actually have to repeat the lie. All you have to do is make a simple gesture such as a head nod or simply say, "Yes." So you psych yourself up and say, "Well, I didn't tell the lie, my friend did." That's where you are wrong! Your desire to be loyal to your friend overrode your morals.

2. Positive Perspective: In this same scenario, it is easy just to go along with the lie, but if you desire to be honest, not even loyalty to a friend will get in the way of that. Your morals will override that

Your friend is testing you, and you are testing your own judgment.

loyalty, hands down! The friend will probably already know where you stand prior to this test. Oh yes, this serves as a test for both you and your friend. Your friend is testing you, and you are testing your own judgment. In the future, the friend will have this test filed in the back of their mind (in that storeroom), and that determines what type or category of friend you fall under. If you lie, you will be under the category of **loose behavior**. This friend can be a bit more immoral around you. If you are honest, you will fall under the category of **respectful**. The friend will not do immoral acts around you—at least not openly, not without feeling ashamed. We have all fallen victim to one or both sides of this coin at some point in our lives. It may have been innocent, where all parties involved

> *We have all fallen victim to one or both sides of this coin at some point in our lives.*

knew that it was a joke. At the end of the day, the same underlying message is still there.

You may be saying, "All of that thought does not go into just asking someone to vouch for you." Well, I beg to differ! Remember that ole dusty storeroom called the subconscious mind?

Remember when I said that thoughts will run in the background, similar to elevator music? It's just playing its little tune, not trying to make too much of a wave, minding its own little business—or so you think. What is really happening is that a seed is being planted.

Here is an example: there may be a song that you hear on the radio. It's not particularly a song that you like; you may even change the channel when you hear it. After

It always comes out at the right (or sometimes at the wrong) time.

hearing it play on the radio a few times, you realize that you now know the words, but you don't even know when it happened. You didn't even like the song!

Well, your subconscious mind had that song stored in that little box back in the corner, on top of that larger box, inside that storeroom. The thoughts can be brought to remembrance when needed. It always comes out at the right (or sometimes at the wrong) time.

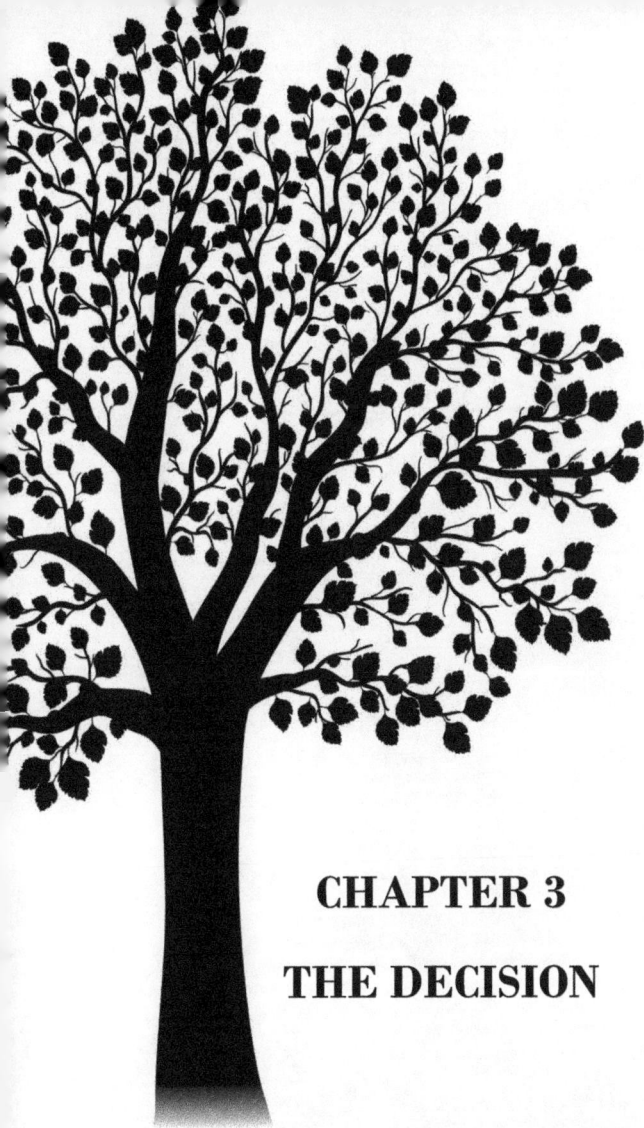

CHAPTER 3

THE DECISION

"For I know that in me dwelleth no good thing: for to will is present with me; but to perform that which is good I find not."

~ ROMANS 7:18

Now this is the very moment that your will either allows you to trust yourself when it comes to making decisions or not to trust your own decisions at a later time and date. This type of situation ties back to why I accepted a lot of negative behavior. When I said I thought that I deserved that type of behavior, it was because at different points in my life, I

This type of situation ties back to why I accepted a lot of negative behavior.

took the wrong road, which led me not to trust my own decisions. A little part in the very back of my mind, my subconscious mind, said, "Girl, you don't even know what's good for you. Look at who you chose to be with!" Now shame seeped into that same area of the brain, and I was too ashamed to speak out against the negative behavior (nothing but the devil). The thought may be, "If you allowed it once, what is different now? It **only** happened that time because..." That is when the cycle continued—until I made a conscious decision to stop the cycle. **When you want to...you gone to!**

Remember when I mentioned previously that everything around me told me that cheating was acceptable? You do? Great! Well, play close attention now! This is when

> *The thought may be, "If you allowed it once, what is different now?*

those things played a major role in developing my mindset. From music to TV to my crowd and even to the experience of being the byproduct of my dad cheating on his wife with my mother—oh, did I forget to mention that earlier? (Yep...close your mouth!) That's an entire book on its own as well. But think about what role that must have played on my mentality. Just that alone, know-ing that as a fact, made me feel like a mistake and ashamed. I couldn't identify it at that time. As a matter of fact, if you would have asked me then, I would have told you that I was perfectly fine. I didn't associate my low self-esteem as being connected to anything in particular, let alone connecting it to my dad. I loved him because I didn't lack for anything that I needed. This may be why I felt secure in choosing a man that provided but was a cheater as a husband.

> *I didn't associate my low self-esteem as being connected to anything in particular, let alone connecting it to my dad.*

At the same time, I hated my dad because he did not plan to come clean to his wife about his little secret. Oh yeah, he didn't tell his wife about his adult daughter (me) until decades later (yep, close your mouth)! In turn, this began a love-hate cycle that I had toward my dad. I think it instilled in me at a young age a spirit of sneakiness, a spirit of untruthfulness or lying. I was taught to accept their deceitfulness. Once again, I did not know what to call it; I just knew that it did not feel good.

Also, I felt that my situation was so unique, at least to my circle, and that no one understood my situation or me. Therefore, how can anyone fix it? After all, I didn't know what the problem was. I did know that I wanted to feel wanted. I wanted to be chosen. I wanted to feel special. I thought feeling wanted would soothe that pain or fill that void. So I felt isolated and alone—not in company but in spirit and in my heart, which in turn began a cycle of not feeling worthy, not

> *I thought feeling wanted would soothe that pain or fill that void.*

trusting my own decisions, and accepting others' poor decision-making for me. This led me down the long, dark road of becoming a teenage mom, a young unhappy wife, a divorcee, a young black single mother, just to name a few.

When I think about it now, I think I just went with others' decisions for me because I felt that I didn't really have a mind of my own, or rather I didn't have the courage to recognize and respect my thoughts. I appeared to be confident to the average onlooker. As I mentioned before, I did not even realize that all of this turmoil was going on in my mind. With the Lord's help, all of that lost time has been made up for! He has given me grace and mercy to walk in a new light! In His light! Thank you, God, for deliverance and for leading me on a new path! **God wanted to save me, so guess what? He did!**

The wrong road of life many times has a bright neon sign that leads you down Back Alley, which is right next to Unimportant Lane, which runs parallel to Almost Road that intersects Later Drive.

> *This is where dreams are parked and forgotten, each street being a dead end.*

This is where dreams are parked and forgotten, each street being a dead end. There is no GPS signal in this neighborhood. There are no streetlights nor sidewalks. The roads are not paved, so you wander around tirelessly, hoping to find your way out, with no true belief that you ever will—until one day the light from that neon sign catches your eye like it never has before. You think to yourself, "If that is the way I came in, why don't I follow that sign back out?" It's the obvious thing to do, but for some reason you did not even consider it a thought prior.

Anticipation builds the closer you get to that neon sign. The colors become a blur as you stare at it so as not to lose it, like so many times before. The thought crosses your mind, "How

> *It's the obvious thing to do, but for some reason you did not even consider it a thought prior.*

did I miss this sign every other day? Was it really here this entire time?" Now your heart is racing because you can smell the fresh air on the other side of that sign. Your desire for fresh air is so urgent that you feel that you could not breathe without it. You need that fresh air. Now, finally at the neon light—finally!—you can breathe.

You see the fork in the road that initially seemed like a one-way street. The good road of life is much more narrow and has a lot less traffic. The good road has bright sunlight with streetlights, sidewalks, nice paved streets with lush trees and bushes. Guess

> *You see the fork in the road that initially seemed like a one-way street.*

what? You even get a strong GPS signal on this side. Your mind cannot believe what you have been missing. But boy are you glad that you finally took that turn! **Finally, you wanted to… so you did!**

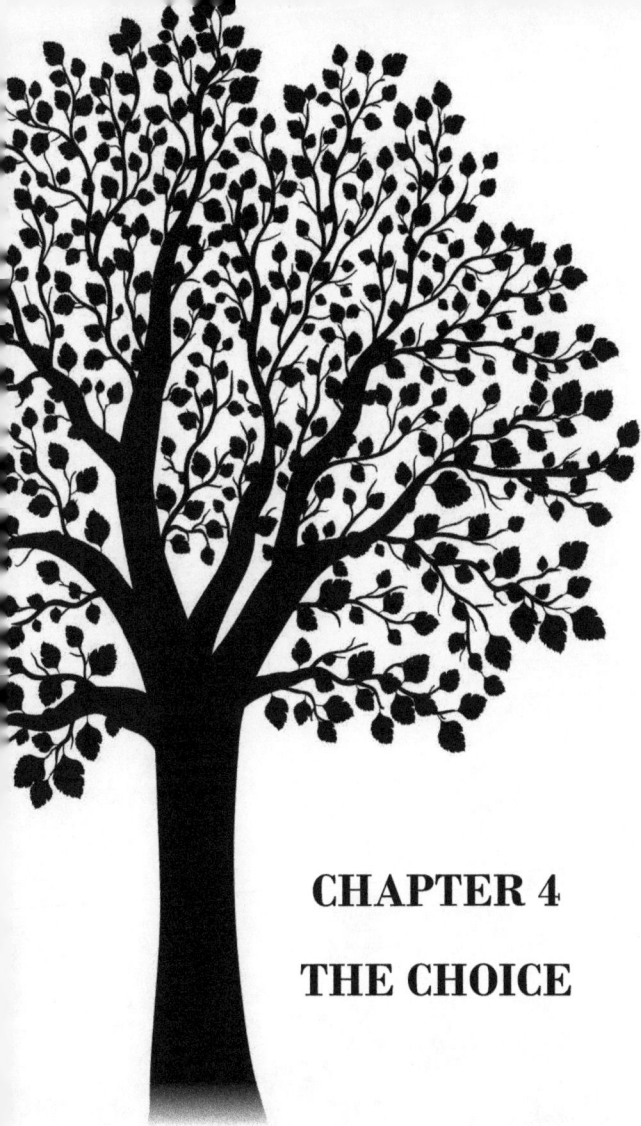

CHAPTER 4

THE CHOICE

"Therefore if any man be in Christ,
he is a new creature, the old things passed
away; behold, all things are become new."

~ 2 Corinthians 5:17

I knew that my mindset was not healthy. I knew that I was ready for a change. I did not know just what to do, but I knew enough to know that what I was doing was not it. I needed to purge my life of impurities. I wasn't sure if I was ready for the "big chop," to do away with everything at once, but change was definitely knocking at my front door. I drew near to God like sheep are

> *I did not know just what to do, but I knew enough to know that what I was doing was not it.*

drawn to their shepherd. I just knew, without convincing, that was what I needed. I had to change all of my outside influences. That meant that I changed where I went, who I went with, what radio station I listened to, the songs I sang, the movies I watched, the activities I participated in. **Literally everything!** I needed my soul to feel clean and pure. A total system wipeout.

Watching TV just didn't really do it for me anymore. As of today, I do not have a TV in my bedroom. I find that the older I get, the less noise I crave. There is solidity in solitude. The difference is that I now value my thoughts and the voice of the Creator. I would even take drives with no radio. Sounds boring, huh? Well, for me it was soul-cleansing. I didn't need the things I once needed because for once I was beginning to finally know who I was.

> *The difference is that I now value my thoughts and the voice of the Creator.*

Guess where I found **her**? She was in that much larger box in the corner underneath the little box in that dusty storeroom of the subconscious mind. All I had to do was remove the little box of "fiery darts," a.k.a. distracting thoughts from the adversary (the devil), that had weighed me down for so long. At that time, it seemed to be a heavy load. Now, I kick that box around with my pinky toe! It's almost laughable now, looking back. I did not know my own strength. Nor did I know whose child I really was. **My Father in heaven is a King! He is the King of Kings!** My earthly

---

But together, they make a beautiful picture—a picture far more grand than my grandest dream!

---

father, along with all of my earthly experiences, are only pieces of my puzzle. Each piece is equally important. They can't all be pretty. But together, they make a beautiful picture—a picture far more grand than my grandest dream! All because I chose to believe that this belongs to me.

So take the first step toward the first step of the dreams that lie dormant in your subconscious mind and in your heart. **Choose to make a choice**. Allow the desires of your heart to flood like a river and overflow into your life and water all of the dry areas of your heart. Allow it to bring light to the dark places and give them life!

This thought mentality that initially began as a slogan for a negative experience that once was my reality I now use as a motto for life. In life there are two modes: doing or not doing; live or die. After choosing the latter for much of my life, I now realize that I control how this story ends. There is freedom in that.

Can I ask you to do something silly with me? Okay, stand to your feet when I count to three. I want you to scream as loud as you can (not yet, we're just practicing):

> *I now realize that I control how this story ends*

Yyyyyeeeeeessssssss!!! I choose life!!! Yyyeeeeessssss!!!

Okay. Are you ready?! On three... One! Two! Three!

Yyyyyeeeeeessssssss!!! I choose life!!! Yyyeeeeesssss!!!

Make any declaration that you like. Write it here:

_____

_____

_____

Take your time. Repeat this as many times as you feel necessary. One more time!

Yyyyyeeeeeessssssss!!! I choose life!!! Yyyeeeeesssss!!!

Wow…that was amazingly powerful! I don't know about you, but I feel ignited! I feel light as a feather! **I feel alive!** Okay, now clear your throat, straighten up your clothes, check your edges, sit back down, and cross your legs. Put that

Put that power in a safe spot.

power in a safe spot. You will need to pull it out

from time to time, just to remind yourself, "I have the power. The power is in me. God has equipped me with everything that I need. Through Him I have strength to do the impossible."

You are equipped with the will and determination to choose your story. The question is, **who are you at your core? What is in your heart of hearts?** At that fork in the road, will you choose the florescent lights flashing from the neon sign? This light goes in and out; the flash is unpredictable.

> *You are equipped with the will and determination to choose your story.*

Someone else can easily pull the plug on this light. Or will you choose the warm natural sunlight? This light is steady and lasts all the day long. This light is a miracle in its own right. It is God-given. No one can ever pull the plug on this light! Which light will you follow? You have the power to choose! **If you want to...you gone to!!!**

CHAPTER 5

THE DIFFERENCE

"For the LORD giveth wisdom:
out of His mouth cometh knowledge."

~ PROVERBS 2:6

Just in case you may be wondering what the difference is between a decision and a choice, by definition, according to The Merriam-Webster Dictionary, a decision is "the act or process of deciding; a determination arrived at after consideration"; a choice, on the other hand, means "the act of choosing (a selection), an option; or care in selecting." **You make a decision to make a choice. You can also choose to make a decision.** The two will usually go hand in hand, but they are in fact different. Here is an example of the difference: I can decide to go shopping without choosing which store I will

> *You make a decision to make a choice. You can also choose to make a decision.*

shop at. I can choose a store and decide not to make a purchase.

I think of it like this: the choice is the supporting factor, while the decision seals the deal. For example, when you have decided to go on a family vacation, the choice is to which destination to travel to. Likewise, one can make a decision on which part of town to purchase a home based

> *I think of it like this: the choice is the supporting factor, while the decision seals the deal.*

on the school system, home prices, and the crime rate, just to name a few. But did they choose what type of neighbor they will be? Choices are made from man's free will. While, decisions are made from reasoning, using facts and figures. A choice can lead up to a decision and support the decision moving forward. A woman can decide to become a mother, but does she really choose what type of mother she will be? Or does she just become a mother of her circumstances? While choosing the type of mother she will be, her choices will support her finale decision. She may choose what she feeds her child, who her child plays with, the style of clothes, and even the toys that she buys for her child. You see, choices usually play out over a longer period of time, while a decision is more of a right-now type of action. Although one decision may alter the future, choices will be made along the way that may alter that outcome. If we were playing Spades, the choice is a spade while the decision is the big joker. Each alone will get you a book,

You see, choices usually play out over a longer period of time, while a decision is more of a right-now type of action. Although one decision may alter the future, choices will be made along the way that may alter that outcome.

but you will likely play multiple spades before pulling out the big joker. The spade (choice) says, "I ain't playing no games." The big joker (decision) says, "Oh, you thought I was playing! I'll show you better than I can tell you! Take this whooping today so you'll know better the next time!"

Oh, you didn't know about the subliminal messages sent during Spades? Well...I digress (with my church finger up)...but if you play your cards just right and finally let that big joker hit the card table... aw, man! You will be respected and requested when it comes to playing

> *You will be respected and requested for the level of wisdom and knowledge that you hold.*

Spades. This concept is much like life: if we allow our decisions and choices to be spirit-led, it will be noticed. You will be respected and requested for the level of wisdom and knowledge that you hold. So think about things that you want to do, the things that you have long desired that you will finally do. Because at the end of the day...if you want to...you gone to!

If They Want to… They Gone to

PERSONAL REFLECTIONS

_____

_____

_____

_____

_____

_____

_____

_____

_____

_____

_____

_____

_____

_____

_____

_____

_____

_____

_____

_____

PERSONAL REFLECTIONS

_____

_____

_____

_____

_____

_____

_____

_____

_____

_____

_____

_____

_____

_____

_____

_____

_____

_____

_____

_____

If They Want to…They Gone to

PERSONAL REFLECTIONS

_____
_____
_____
_____
_____
_____
_____
_____
_____
_____
_____
_____
_____
_____
_____
_____
_____
_____
_____
_____

ACKNOWLEDGMENTS

———◆◆◆———

There are so many amazing people in my life. Each and every one of them are equally as important to me in different ways. Thank you all for enjoying this journey called life with me.

To my kids, Deizha, Dominique, and Derrick (DJ), it has been a joy parenting the three of you through the different stages of your lives.

To my mom for being my constant rock through it all.

To my pastors at the Bridge Church of Pearl, MS, Pastors Jamane and Alecia Williams. Your leadership has been instrumental to my growth.

To my close circle of family and friends, you all have witnessed my evolution through life and all that comes with it.

Thank you all for every prayer, every laugh, every word of encouragement, and every memory!

ABOUT THE AUTHOR

———◆———

Shavon A. Hampton is a new author and founder of Novahs Publishing LLC (www.novaahspublishing.com) located in Jackson, MS, where she is also a native. She is a respiratory therapist (RRT) at a state trauma center, also located in Jackson. She has a passion for creativity of all forms. She enjoys deep conversation, baking, and being in nature near water.

Shavon is a mother of three and a Mimi to one. She is also a woman of faith who continues to strengthen her journey to be more Christlike.

You can follow Shavon on Facebook and Instagram @*shavonhamptonspeaks*.

You can also visit her website at
www.shavonhampton.life.